I'm Moving to Mars!

by Mrs. Savoia's and Miss Gratton's classes with Tony Stead

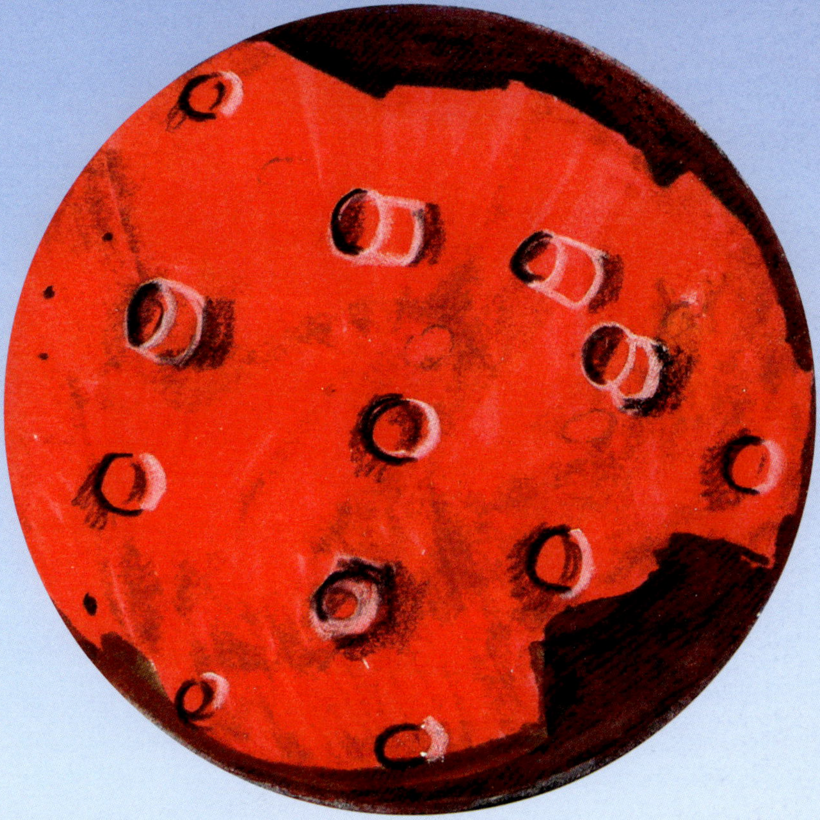

capstone

Introduction

by Nicole

What would it be like to live on Mars? When our fifth grade classes thought about this topic we came up with many different answers. We decided to research this topic to learn as much as we could about the red planet called Mars. Now our classes are experts, and you will be, too!

Earth vs. Mars

by May

The planet Mars is very far from Earth. The minimum distance is 35 million miles away. Sometimes it is even further away. Not only is it far from Earth, but it is also very different from Earth. Read on to find out how!

The Atmosphere

We know that Earth is full of life. In contrast, spacecraft have not found signs of life on Mars yet. The air on Mars is impossible for humans to breathe. It is mainly made of carbon dioxide. There is no oxygen. The surface of Mars looks hot because it is red, but it's actually freezing cold. It averages around -81 degrees Fahrenheit.

How High Can You Jump on Mars?

Mars's gravity is only 37 percent of Earth's gravity. You could leap nearly three times higher on Mars than on Earth. I would like to jump that high!

The Red Dust

Mars is covered in red dust, which rises with the air and causes great dust storms. Storms on Mars are much different from storms on Earth. The dust storms last for weeks on end. Some of them can also affect all of the planet. Imagine if a massive storm covered the whole planet, not just your town, not just your country, but the whole planet! That's what it's like! The dust storms are powered by sunshine. The sunshine heats up the dust, which makes it lift up and make a dust storm.

Earth vs. Mars		
	Earth	**Mars**
Life	Lots of life	Not found yet
Surface Temp	-126/136 (min/max) °F	-225 to +70 °F
Moons	One moon	Two moons
Air	Mainly nitrogen and oxygen	Mainly carbon dioxide

The Moons of Mars

Earth has only one moon while Mars has two, Phobos and Deimos. Phobos means "fear," and Deimos means "flight." They are both named after sons of the Greek war god, Ares. Phobos and Deimos were studied in 1971 by an American astronomer.

Earth and Mars are very different, especially in temperature, gravity, number of moons, and atmosphere.

The two moons of Mars are much smaller than Earth's moon.

Mars in the Solar System

by Danai

Mars is the fourth planet from the sun. It is a very active planet like Earth. It has evidence of volcanoes and water in the past. With all of their similarities, Mars is not much like Earth.

What Is the Solar System?

The solar system is a group of planets that orbits the sun. Earth is the third planet from the sun and Mars is the fourth.

What Does Mars Look Like?

Mars is often called "the red planet." Its reddish color comes from the high amount of iron oxide on the surface. Mars has mountain ranges, volcanic mountains, valleys, ice-caps, canyons, and deserts.

The Mars rover takes pictures of what the planet looks like and sends them back to Earth.

How Big is Mars?

Mars is much smaller than Earth. This table shows that Mars is about half the size of Earth, and the land area of Earth is about the same area of the whole planet of Mars. Earth also has about ten times more mass and six times more volume than Mars.

	Mars	**Earth**
Diameter	6, 779 kilometers	12,742 kilometers
Surface Area	144 million km^2	510 million km^2
Mass	642 sextillion kg	5972 sextillion kg
Volume	163 billion km^3	260 billion km^3

As you can see, Mars is very different from Earth, even though some things are the same. It is also a far-away planet.

illustrated by Nicole

Mars and Its Moons

By Talia

Have you ever thought about Mars' moons and how many moons Mars has? First of all, do you even know what a moon is? Actually, there is not just one definition to what a moon is, but there are some common things that they share.

Moons are whole and come in all different shapes and sizes. A moon orbits around a more massive body. For example, our moon's orbit takes 29.5 days. You might have thought of moons as round, large objects. However, the moons of Mars are irregularly shaped.

Did you know that moons are also known as satellites? A satellite can be any object that circles a larger object. Well, you just learned something new! Mars has two moons. Their names are Phobos and Deimos.

Phobos and Deimos are smaller than Mars. They orbit the planet, which is bigger than they are. So they are Mars' moons!

Phobos
Deimos

What's the Temperature Like on Mars?

By Gianna

Did you know that the temperature of a planet depends more on its distance from the sun? Mars is a very cold planet and is farther away from the sun than Earth. Mars' atmosphere is about 100 times thinner than Earth's. Do you know what that means? Without a thick atmosphere, Mars is unable to keep in heat energy from the sun. Earth's atmosphere is kind of like a coat.

So remember, if you intend on visiting Mars in the future, you would have to wear a special space suit that will keep the cold out and provide you oxygen to breathe. This is because Mars' atmosphere is mostly made up of carbon dioxide, the air you breathe out! That space suit is necessary because Mars can get as cold as -225 degrees Fahrenheit. That's cold! In contrast, on a sunny day, Mars may get up to 70 degrees Fahrenheit near its equator. Because of these extreme temperatures, there is a lot of humidity on Mars.

Mars can be very cold. Not only that but the atmosphere is very thin, so you would not be able to breathe on Mars. Is the planet Mars someplace you would want to travel to?

illustrated by Talia

How Gravity Affects Your Weight on Mars

By Hailey

Have you ever wondered why your weight changes when you are on other planets? Gravity plays a huge role in this matter. In fact, you are lighter on Mars than on Earth.

Weight is the gravitational force of an object. Gravity is a pulling force measured by mass and distance. Mass is the amount of matter in an object. The gravity on Mars is about three times weaker than it is on Earth. That's why you are lighter on Mars than on Earth.

When you're on Mars, your weight changes but your mass will not. Imagine you are out in space away from any gravitational field with a bowling ball in your hands. Let it go and it just floats in front of you. Without gravity, there is no weight. Remember weight changes in space not your mass.

why am I floating ???
Because our weight changes in space

Traveling to Mars

by Jessica L.

Have you ever wondered how you would survive on Mars? Read on to learn how to send the things you need to Mars and what equipment you should bring.

How Would You Send Equipment to Mars?

You would need to send some of your equipment up into space ahead of time because there would not be enough room in the spaceship. The spaceship would be too heavy to take off. You would need to send up supplies separately. You would collect these pieces on Mars.

My idda of what a Spaceship to mars will look like.

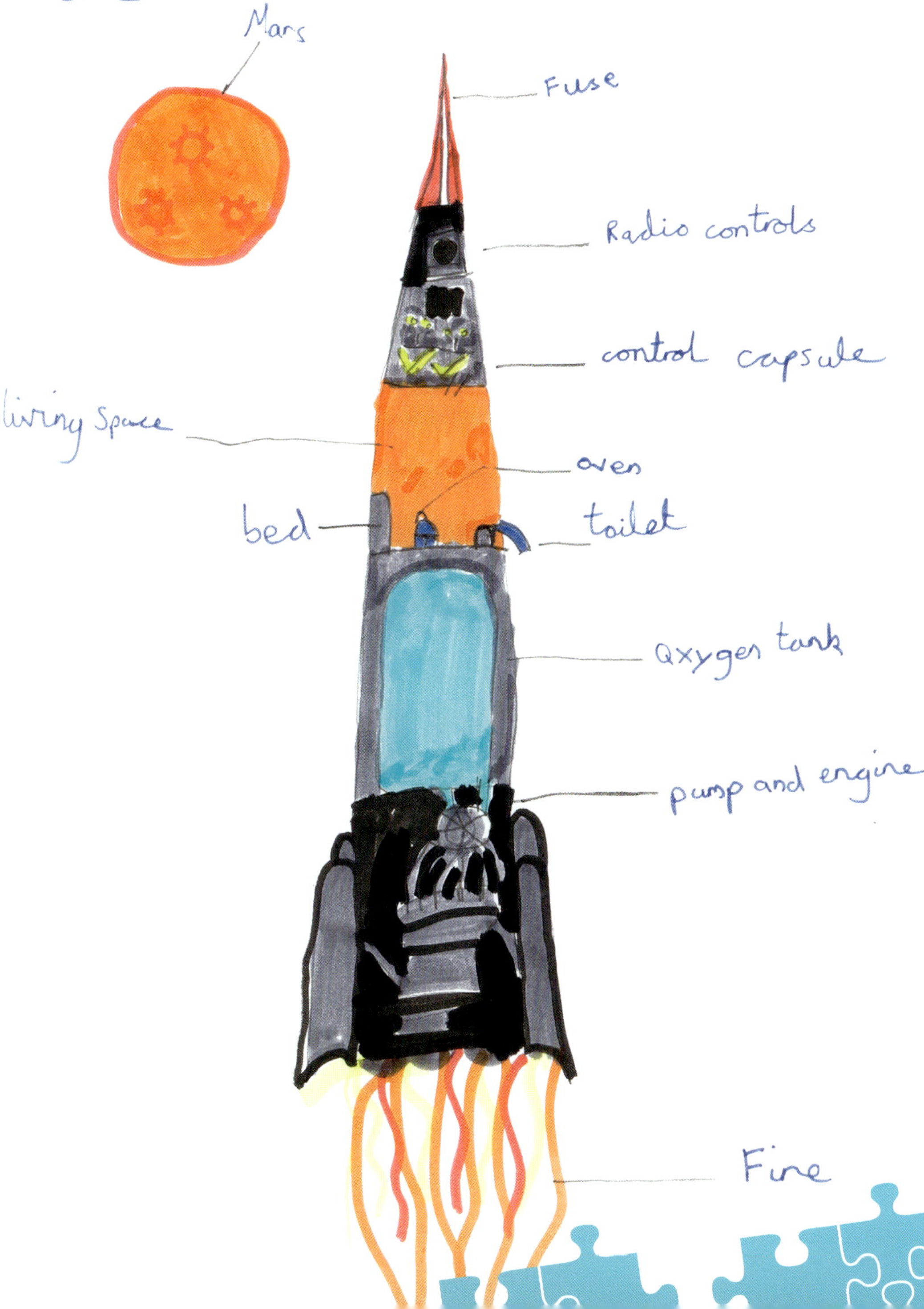

What Should You Take in the Spaceship?

It will take nine months to get to Mars, so you need lots of equipment like:

- Oxygen
- Water
- Food
- A way to land
- A space suit
- Heater
- Tools to collect samples
- Medicine
- A radio for communicating with Earth

As a tip, take the things that you don't have on Mars like sweets and chocolate! And don't forget your space suit. It will help you breathe when you get to Mars.

It's important to make sure you take protective gear, equipment, and sweets. This will help make sure you can survive on Mars and have some treats from home.

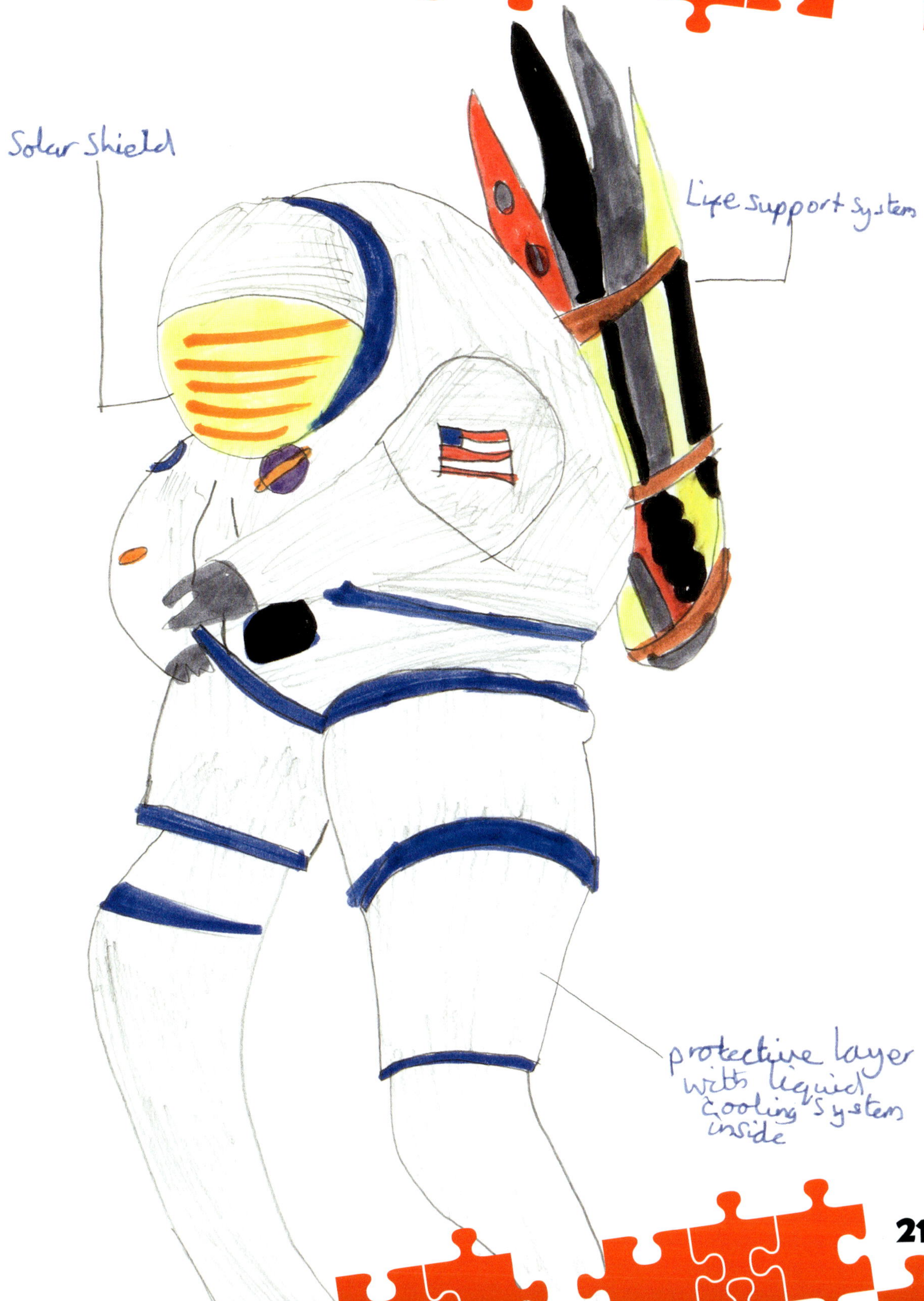
Solar Shield
Life support system
protective layer
with liquid
cooling system
inside

Is There Life on Mars?

By Jessica V.

Long, long ago in the late 1800s, an American astronomer named Percival Lowell studied Mars through his telescope. He thought he saw canals filled with water. People got curious and thought that there might be life on Mars.

Later, rovers (robots) went to Mars to find any past water activity. Using the rovers, we were able to see that there is water on Mars. Using an imaging spectrometer, researchers found changes in Mars' surface that they thought could only be made by water. These darkish streaks appeared over time. They darkened and seemed to flow down steep slopes during warmer seasons and then go away during cooler seasons.

All of these findings contributed to scientists thinking that there might be life on Mars. Lowell was wrong about the canals, but new discoveries show that some form of life on Mars might be possible.

Roaming Rovers: The Only Way to Go

by Ben

Did you ever wonder why we know so much about Mars? Well, I have, too, and I found it very interesting when I researched it. We use rovers and landers, which are unmanned ships, to explore this faraway planet.

Many rovers have been sent to Mars. Spirit was one of the first rovers sent to Mars. Spirit was launched from Cape Canaveral Air Force Station in Florida on June 10, 2003, at 1:58 pm. A few months into the journey, Spirit got hit with a big burst of solar radiation. Solar radiation, or solar flares, is energy radiated from the sun.

Solar flares are common in space, but these flares were the strongest ever recorded! As Spirit neared Mars, scientists were worried that its landing capabilities were damaged. There are many items needed in order to land safely. Thrusters are needed to slow the rover down. Also, the rover's parachute needed to deploy correctly so the rover could drop safely onto Mars. Fortunately, everything worked as needed and the rover successfully landed on Mars.

illustrated by May

At first, Spirit was not responding to mission control. Scientists wondered if Spirit had been damaged. Then, Spirit started sending data back, but it would stop sometimes. Spirit continued to send data on and off for seven years. Spirit really helped NASA scientists find out many unknown things about Mars.

Another rover that successfully landed on Mars was the Curiosity rover. NASA launched Curiosity on November 26, 2011. Curiosity was sent to find out if life or water existed on Mars. It also collected many rock samples from Mars. The rover found evidence of water on Mars just below the planet's surface.

Mars is a faraway planet with many secrets to be discovered. We shall continue to explore Mars, and maybe one day humans will get to land on Mars. What an exciting day that will be!

How Could We Live on Mars?

by Chloe

Many scientists believe that in the future people could leave Earth and live on Mars. Can this really be possible? It is not possible to breathe on Mars. It is far away from help on Earth. So how could humans survive? Let's find out!

To live on Mars you would have to take a lot of helmets. You would need different sizes because you would grow out of them. You would need a special suit to protect you from the sun's radiation. Radiation on Mars is dangerous because Mars doesn't have much of an atmosphere to shield people from it.

Fun Fact

A space suit weighs 280 pounds on Earth, but in space it weighs nothing because there is no gravity out there!

If you have an illness or situation that involves medicine, eventually you would run out of medicine, and you might die! So you would need to take lots of supplies.

Some of the supplies would be used in the lab. On Mars you would need a lab to study information and to communicate with Earth. If something bad happened, it could take several minutes to get a message to Earth, based on how long it took signals from rovers. You would want to make sure you know how to help yourself in case of emergency.

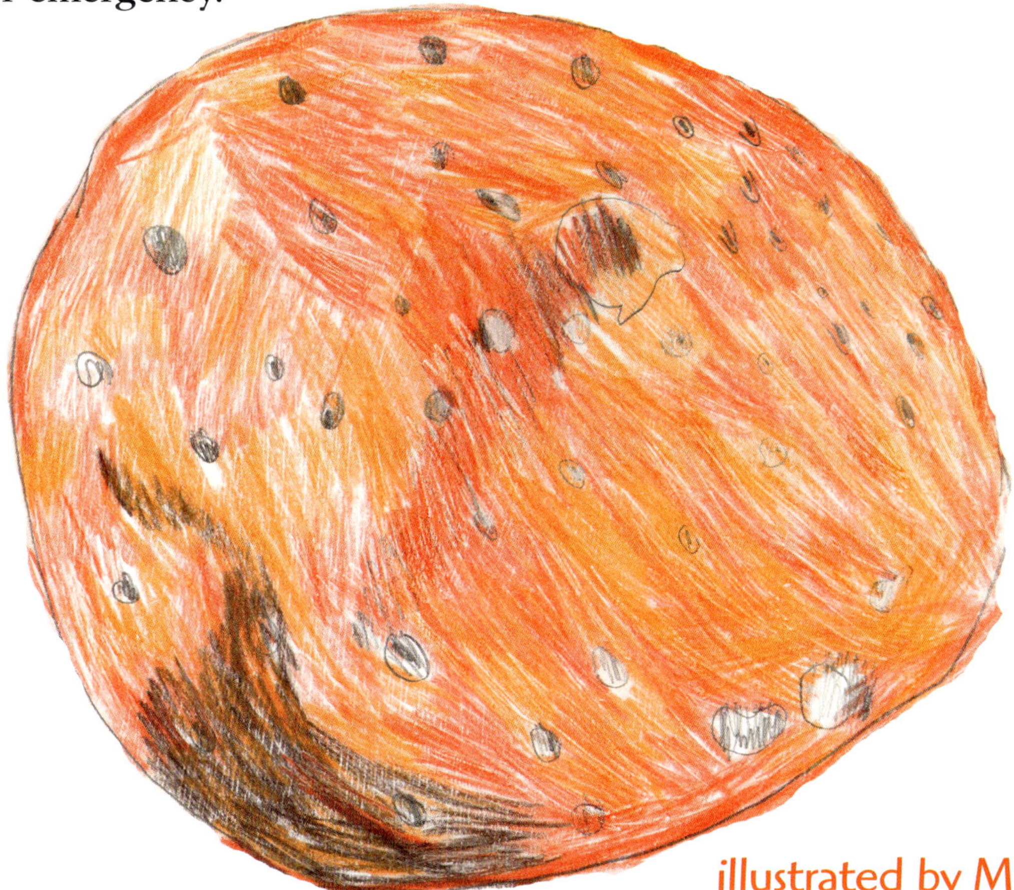

illustrated by May

You also need a biodome to protect you and your belongings, including, air, food, and a place to rest and sleep. You will also need somewhere to train for dangerous storms. That is also when a biodome comes in handy.

It would take a lot of work and supplies to live on Mars! But it would be worth it so that you could see a whole new planet.

Biodome

A biodome is a huge man-made dome that can protect living things. We know that because "bio" means life. From above, the biodome could look like a huge greenhouse. To get in the biodome, you would have to have an airlock to keep all the carbon dioxide out. For example, you would have two doors. You would open the first door and take your suit off except for your helmet because the carbon dioxide would be in that area. So then you would walk through an airlock door and end up in another space.

illustrated by Chloe

Conclusion

We hope this book got you excited to someday travel in space and visit the red planet! At least now you'll have a little information to prepare you for your adventure!